Dresses
Fashion
Coloring Book

This book belongs to

Welcome

A word from the Author

The author has no control over the printing process or paper quality. While this paper is suited for crayons and colored pencils, please use it with caution with markers and I do not advise using it with watercolors or other paints.

The author recommends using a loose sheet of blank paper behind the page you are coloring to avoid any bleed through or accidental transfer.

Thank you and I hope you enjoy coloring this book.

Thank you

... for buying this coloring book,
and I hope you had as much fun
coloring the pages as
I had making it.

If you enjoyed this book,
please don't forget
to leave a review
on Amazon.

Just a simple and
quick review will
help me a lot.

Scan me

For your convenience,
please scan the QR code
from your cellphone and you will
be taken directly to Amazon.

Thank you

... for buying this coloring book, and I hope you had as much fun coloring the pages as I had making it.

If you enjoyed this book, please don't forget to leave a review on Amazon.

Just a simple and quick review will help me a lot.

Scan me

For your convenience, please scan the QR code from your cellphone and you will be taken directly to Amazon.

Made in United States
Orlando, FL
09 May 2023

32965420R00061